Sainte-Marie among the Hurons

Sainte~Marie among the Hurons

Text by Barbara McConnell

Photographs by Michael Odesse

Toronto
OXFORD UNIVERSITY PRESS
1980

ACKNOWLEDGEMENTS

In writing the Introduction I have been greatly assisted by two valuable scholarly articles: Cornelius J. Jaenen, 'Amerindian Views of French Culture in the Seventeenth Century', *Canadian Historical Review*, vol. LV, no. 3, September 1974; and Bruce G. Trigger, 'The French Presence in Huronia: The Structure of Franco-Huron Relations in the First Half of the Seventeenth Century', *Canadian Historical Review*, vol. XLIX, no. 2, June 1965. Quotations are from *The Works of Samuel de Champlain* (6 vols, Toronto, 1922-36) edited by H.P. Biggar and the *Jesuit Relations and Allied Documents* (74 vols, Cleveland, 1896-1901) edited by R.G. Thwaites.

   I wish to express my appreciation to the following people for their help and encouragement: Gail Lindale, whose site manual for Sainte-Marie among the Hurons was invaluable; Michele Quealey, the librarian of the Huronia Historical Parks resource library at Sainte-Marie; John Court; Robert Montgomery; and William Toye of the Oxford University Press.

B.M. McCONNELL
November 1979

Canadian Cataloguing in Publication Data

McConnell, Barbara.
   Sainte-Marie among the Hurons

ISBN 0-19-540306-1

1. Fort Ste. Marie, Ont. I. Odesse, Michael.
II. Title.
FC321.M23   971.01′62   C80-094075-X
F1030.7.M23

Designed by *Fortunato Aglialoro*
© Oxford University Press (Canadian Branch) 1980
ISBN 0-19-5403061
1 2 3 4 - 3 2 1 0
Printed in Hong Kong by
EVERBEST PRINTING COMPANY LIMITED

Introduction
by Barbara McConnell

Beside the little river called the Wye, just before it empties into Georgian Bay half a mile to the north, was the first inland European settlement north of Mexico, the residence of the Jesuit missionaries to the Huron Indians. Sainte-Marie-aux-pays-des-Hurons—or Sainte-Marie among the Hurons, as it is called in English—was a palisaded community of some twenty buildings set in a marshy plain surrounded by an almost impenetrable forest and scattered Indian villages joined by footpaths. It was nearly a month's journey from Quebec—'at the extreme end of the world', in the words of Father Vimont. Though it had a relatively brief existence, from 1639 to 1649, Sainte-Marie represents a spectacular episode in the history of New France when some ardent apostles bravely erected a crude manifestation of European culture among a Stone Age people, and against this backdrop enacted a dramatic story of visionary zeal, suffering, toil, accomplishment, and failure. Its monument exists today in the form of an extensive reconstruction.

The story can begin with Samuel de Champlain, who visited the region of the Hurons in 1615, seven years after he had founded Quebec. He had come to Huronia, between present-day Georgian Bay and Lake Simcoe in central Ontario, by way of the Ottawa and Mattawa Rivers, Lake Nipissing, and French River. With two Frenchmen and ten Indians he had paddled down Georgian Bay and reached Huronia, near Penetanguishene, on August 1st. Here, where the land was 'so fine and fertile it is a pleasure to travel in it', he found the Hurons—there were some 30,000 of them—living in semi-permanent villages and bartering corn and squash, which they grew, with northern and western tribes for game, fish, and furs.

> Now in all these villages they received us very courteously with some modest welcome. This whole region which I visited on foot extends for some twenty or thirty leagues, and is very fine, being in latitude 44° 33', and a well cleared country where they plant much Indian corn, which comes up very well, as do also squashes and sunflowers, from the seeds of which they make oil wherewith they annoint their heads. The region is crossed by many streams which empty into the lake [Huron] .... And this small extent of territory I have observed to be well peopled with a countless number of souls, without reckoning the other districts which I did not visit, which by common report are as thickly settled as those above mentioned, or more so; and I reflected that it is a great

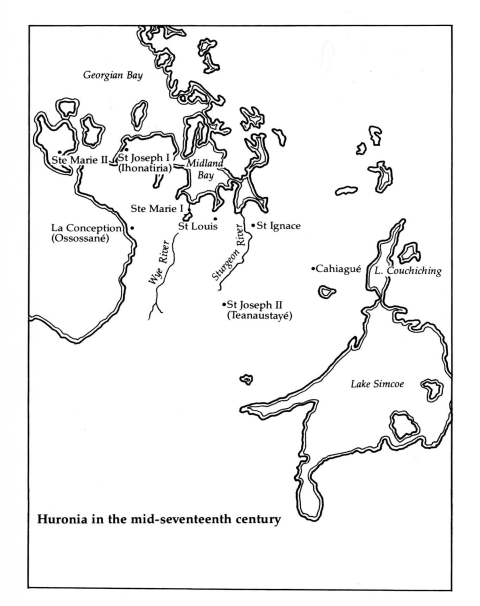

Huronia in the mid-seventeenth century

misfortune that so many poor creatures should live and die without any knowledge of God and even without any religion or law, whether divine, political or civil, established among them. (Champlain, *Works*, III, 50-1)

Every spring since Quebec had been established as a trading post, the Hurons had travelled there to obtain European goods in exchange for furs. Living in a crucial and compact middle ground between the fur-bearing regions in the northwest and the St Lawrence, they were obviously important to the development of the fur trade and Champlain wanted to cultivate their friendship. He spent a month with them, going from one village to another.

His regret that the Hurons would die 'without any knowledge of God' anticipated a policy of the French crown to strengthen ties with the Hurons and at the same time save their souls for God. These sedentary Indians seemed to be ideal candidates for Christianization. As early as 1615 two Recollet priests were sent to Huronia as missionaries, and others followed. But such efforts showed few results until after 1633, when the Society of Jesus took charge of missionary activities in New France. Father Jean de Brébeuf was made superior of the Huron missions in 1634 and he established the mission of Saint-Joseph at Ihonatiria. In 1637 another mission, La Conception, was founded at Ossossané; the following year Saint-Joseph was moved to Teanaustayé.

In 1638 Jean de Brébeuf was succeeded as superior by Father Jérôme Lalemant, who decided that the work of the missionaries required a headquarters that would exist apart from the Indian villages as a refuge and a place of rest and meditation for the priests who worked with the Indians. Choosing a site on the Wye River in 'the heart of all our missions', he founded Sainte-Marie-aux-pays-des-Hurons. In the next few years the labour of craftsmen brought from Quebec and France created a little enclave of wooden buildings of European design that was separated by 800 miles of wilderness from Quebec and Trois-Rivières. Beginning with a residence and chapel for the priests, Sainte-Marie grew to include a church, a hospital, workshops, a stable, barns, a cookhouse, a kitchen garden, and dwellings for lay workers and Indian converts; it was fortified by a log palisade with stone bastions. Cattle, pigs, and poultry were brought by canoe from Quebec and fields were cleared to grow corn, beans, and squash.

1   Two manuscript pages from a letter by Jérôme Lalemant, 1642

The Indians often travelled clear across their country to watch the Frenchmen raise a building. They wondered what motivated them to build such a substantial community when fire or soil depletion necessitated *their* relocation every decade or so. But the Jesuits did not build solely for their comfort and protection. They wanted Sainte-Marie to be an example of French culture and Christian living for the Indians.

For the two or three priests who were in sole charge at Sainte-Marie through most of the year, the day began with devotions at 4 a.m. These lasted for four hours. After morning Mass and breakfast, the gates were opened to the Indians who came for religious instruction, medical attention, or food. The priests spent mornings and afternoons, with a break for the noon meal, working with them. In the background of these activities, craftsmen and domestics were performing *their* duties: constructing or repairing buildings, fashioning tools and furniture, making clothes, cooking, gardening, tending crops and animals, cutting firewood. When the chapel bell rang for Mass at 4 p.m., the non-Christian Indians were asked to leave. The evening meal was at 6 or 6:30 p.m. and everyone retired around 8 p.m. Once a year, for a month, the Europeans at Sainte-Marie joyfully welcomed a little influx of Jesuits from the outlying Indian villages who had come for their annual retreat. This took place in the summer because it was then that the Huron men were away fishing, hunting, or on warring expeditions and the women were off with their children tending the cornfields, which were often several miles away from a village. For many of the missionary-priests this was the only time they could meet and talk with others of their kind. The retreats were therefore happy occasions, but it was never forgotten that they were primarily times for gathering physical and, more important, spiritual strength for the coming year.

When they first came to Huronia the Jesuits were rather patronizing towards the Hurons among whom they lived—though their use of the word 'savages' (*sauvages*) or 'barbarians' (*barbares*) to refer to the Indians did not signify disrespect. Attempting to impose their concepts and values on them, the priests failed to understand that the Hurons had their own values, conventions, and religion. But they eventually saw their mistake and began to accept the fact that they must build on Huron beliefs. They realized that they were in Huronia on sufferance. Initially the Indians feared the Jesuits as sorcerers and rejected their teachings; they did not comprehend the priests' attempts to supplant their own religion and undermine all the things they believed. However, they were willing to put up with the missionaries because they wanted to continue the benefits of trading with the French—though some Hurons became violently resentful. Between 1635 and 1640 the Indians were ravaged by influenza and an epidemic of smallpox. (By 1640 epidemics, famine, and warfare had reduced their population by half.) They noticed that the priests' hasty baptisms of the hopelessly ill were often immediately followed by death. There were riots and the priests were vilified. After the epidemic had run its course, however, more and more Hurons found reasons to adopt Christianity. Whether attracted by the ritual and ceremony of the Catholic religion, the stoicism and compassion of the Jesuits, the culture they represented, or thinking that to become Christian would advance them in the eyes of the French at Quebec, they underwent conversion.

A series of annual reports, written in the form of letters to the superiors in France and published as the *Jesuit Relations*, describes the work of the missionary-priests. We read of their stoic acceptance of abuse and physical discomfort; their often ill-founded claims that the Hurons were responding sympathetically to their teachings; their almost eager acceptance of the possibility of martyrdom; their painstaking attempts to understand the natives, learn their language, and adapt themselves to their ways. One of Father Lalemant's reports describes Sainte-Marie in 1641-2:

OF THE HOUSE OR PERMANENT RESIDENCE OF SAINTE MARIE
We have numbered this Year here among the Hurons, fourteen Priests of our Society; but we hardly ever meet all together for a whole month at a time. We are generally scattered, especially during Winter, which is the most important season of work for the conversion of these Peoples. Eight of the number found their employment in the four principal Huron Missions which we have been able to maintain this Year. The Algonquins who dwell here, near our Hurons, have occupied the attention of three others. Our Fathers being thus distributed, each having charge of the Mission that has fallen to his share, I have been obliged to join them—sometimes for a month at one place, then in another, as the occasion presented itself; therefore, I have had no fixed abode. Consequently, the care of this Residence has been shared by the only two who remained—Father Isaac Jogues and Father François du Peron.

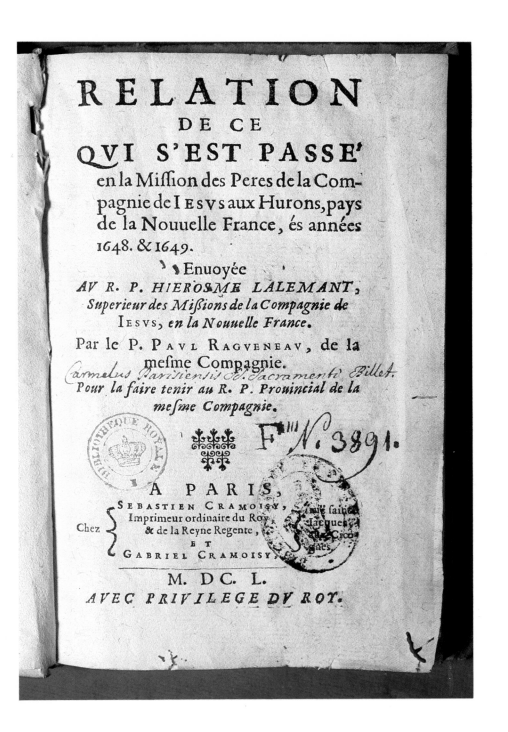

2 Title page of the *Jesuit Relations* for 1648-9 (Paris, 1650)

It is a profound consolation to all our Missionaries, after the fatigues of the Winter or of the Summer, to return to this House, in order to give some attention to themselves, and to breathe a little more freely with God in tranquillity of spirit, that they may return afterwards to the same work with renewed vigor. In addition to this, they derive marked benefit from the conferences that they hold, all together, not only in the enlightenment and the methods disclosed to them by God to facilitate the instruction and Conversion of the Savages, but in the new knowledge they have acquired for their advancement in a Language in which one must be both Master and Pupil at the same time.

As this House is the centre of the country, it frequently has the consolation of receiving the Christians who come to it from various places, to perform their Devotions in more quiet than in the Villages, and in this sort of Solitude to entertain, at greater leisure, sentiments of Piety and Religion. For that purpose we have prepared for them a Refuge or Cabin of bark, wherein God gives us the means of lodging and feeding these good Pilgrims in their own Country. During the Summer, from fortnight to fortnight, there are always a goodly number who come to it on Saturday, from a distance of four or five leagues, to pass the Sunday in a devout manner, leaving only on Monday morning. On the following Sunday, we save them this trouble; for our Fathers go to their houses a day or two beforehand, to prepare them for the Devotions of that holy Day. Thus, by these alternate visits, we gently maintain them in the practice of Christianity, whereof during the Winter, while we reside more constantly with them, we have endeavored to give them more substantial knowledge.

If in the Missions some Adult in good health is deemed worthy of Baptism, after all the trials to which he is subjected, he is sent to this House to be again examined, and to receive with solemnity that Sacrament which makes him a Child of the Church.

We have reserved the majority of these Baptisms for the Festivals of Christmas, of Easter, and of Pentecost, from which our Christians, who have assembled there from all parts, have always departed with a marked increase in their faith. The outward splendour with which we endeavor to surround the Ceremonies of the Church; the beauty of our Chapel (which is looked upon in this Country as one of the Wonders of the World, although in France it would be considered but a poor affair); the Masses, Sermons, Vespers, Processions, and Benedictions of the Blessed Sacrament that are said and celebrated at such times, with a magnificence surpassing anything that the eyes of our Savages have ever beheld —all these things produce an impression on their minds, and give them an idea of the Majesty of God, who, we tell them, is honored throughout the World by a worship a thousand times more imposing. (JR XXIII, 19-23)

In the meantime the French-Huron alliance that directed a profitable flow of furs to Quebec had received a serious set-back from the Mohawks, one of the five nations of the Iroquois confederacy who lived south of Lake Ontario. They had been trading with the Dutch on the Hudson River and had exhausted their own fur regions. They tried to set up a trading alliance with the Hurons, but when nothing came of this they turned their attention to the cargoes of furs that were brought annually to Quebec from the northwest. With great daring and effectiveness they ambushed the Huron canoe-fleets, carrying off the furs to their own territory. Between 1640 and 1645 they blockaded the Ottawa River route and attacked the settlements along the St Lawrence. Then they sought to divert the annual supply of furs from the northwest to the Dutch. They embarked on a series of attacks on Huronia itself with the apparent intention of eliminating their rivals in the fur trade.

Father Brébeuf wrote on June 2nd, 1648, while he was the mission priest at Sainte-Marie:

. . . there are, altogether, many and considerable influences which not only hinder our work, but seem even to threaten the ruin of the whole mission. Some of these, indeed, are common to us with all the Hurons—especially the enemy, whom we call by the name of Iroquois; they, on one hand, close the roads and obstruct trade, and, on the other, devastate this region by frequent massacre; in short, they fill every place with fear. Other hindrances, however, are altogether peculiar to us—notably, the hatred toward us of certain infidel Hurons, which has grown to the degree that a few days ago they killed one of our domestics [Jacques Douart]. They were ready to offer the same treatment to us, if opportunity had occurred. (JR XXXII, 61)

The murder of Jacques Douart occurred because some Hurons continued to oppose the intrusion of the Jesuits and everything they

3 *Donnés* paddling on the Wye River

4 Sainte-Marie (Northcourt) from the Wye River.

5 *(over)* Approaching the entrance to the mission.

stood for, fearful of the changes they were bringing about. This faction was led by certain chiefs who wanted to save their traditional culture and at the same time put an end to Iroquois depredations. They would have done this by breaking the alliance with the French, expelling the Jesuits, and trading with the Iroquois. The killing of Douart by two Hurons was apparently approved by the anti-French chiefs, who wanted to force the issue of whether the French should be sent out of Huronia and the Iroquois appeased. At a council meeting afterwards, their side lost to the faction that desired to remain friendly with the French. A gift of one hundred beaver skins was presented to the Jesuits in compensation for the murder.

In July 1648 the Iroquois (Senecas) attacked Saint-Joseph and the village was destroyed. Father Antoine Daniel was shot with arrows and some 700 Hurons were killed.

> *The house of Saint Marie has been, until now [1648], in the heart of the country, and has, therefore, been less exposed to the inroads of the enemy. It is true that, from time to time, some venturesome foes have come to strike an evil blow within sight of our settlement; but they did not dare to approach, except in small numbers and in secret, lest they might be perceived from the frontier villages, and attacked. We have lived in sufficient security on that score, and, thank God, not one of us has yet been surprised in their ambushes.*
>
> *We are forty-two Frenchmen in the midst of all these infidel Nations—eighteen being of our Society [priests and lay brothers], while the remainder are chosen persons [donnés], most of whom have resolved to live and to die with us; they assist us by their labor and industry with a courage, a faithfulness, and a holiness that assuredly are not of earth. (JR XXXIII, 75)*

When Saint-Joseph was destroyed, terror struck the other villages. Thousands of Indians took refuge at Sainte-Marie.

> *This house is a resort for the whole Country, where the Christians find a Hospital in their sicknesses, a refuge in the height of alarms, and a hospice when they come to visit us. During the past year, we have reckoned over three thousand persons to whom we have given shelter—sometimes within a fortnight, six or seven hundred Christians; and, as a rule, three meals to each one. This does not include a*

> *larger number who incessantly come hither to pass the whole day, and to whom we also give charity. (JR XXXIII, 77)*

In March 1649 the Iroquois came back a thousand strong, armed with guns. They attacked and demolished Saint-Louis and Saint-Ignace. (Smoke from the flames at Saint-Ignace, eleven miles away, could be seen from Sainte-Marie.) Fathers Brébeuf and Gabriel Lalemant were captured at Saint-Louis, tortured, and killed at Saint-Ignace.

The destruction of Huronia was complete when most of the demoralized survivors fled their country or surrendered to the Iroquois. Seeing the obliteration of all their hopes for the Huron mission, the Jesuits decided to abandon Sainte-Marie. With several hundred Christian Indian families they moved to Saint-Joseph Island (Christian Island) in Georgian Bay.*

> *We, the Shepherds, followed our fleeing flock, and we too have left our dwelling-place—I might call it our delight—the residence of Sainte Marie, and the fields we had tilled, which promised a rich harvest. Nay, more, we even applied the torch to the work of our own hands, lest the sacred House should furnish shelter to our impious enemy; and thus in a single day, and almost in a moment, we saw consumed our work of nearly ten years, which had given us the hope that we could produce the necessities of life, and thus maintain ourselves in this country without aid from France. But God has willed otherwise; our home is now laid waste. (JR XXXV, 25)*

Thus a brave missionary endeavour came to an end. Over the next few months a once-populous region of Indian settlements and cultivated fields was stripped not only of the Hurons but of every vestige of their life there.

THE MISSIONARIES AND THEIR HELPERS

The work of the missionaries in Huronia had the approval of the French crown because it seemed to support the government's commercial interests in New France by maintaining good relations with the

---

*A shortage of food and the starvation that resulted caused them to abandon that settlement too the next spring. The priests, with some 300 Hurons, returned to Quebec.

Hurons. But for the Jesuits themselves there was only one objective: to save the souls of the Indians by converting them to Christianity. Once they embarked on this mission the priests withstood almost unendurable hardships, not only during the nearly month-long trip to the Huron villages but thereafter—especially during the grim months of winter.

Of all the Jesuits who served in the Huron country, the most popular was Father Brébeuf, who spent longer there than the others and truly thrived until he met his violent end. A tall, robust, happy man who was down-to-earth in his everyday conduct but mystically inclined where his faith was concerned, he was loved by both the Hurons and his fellow Frenchmen. His delicate understanding of the Indians and his total dedication are vividly conveyed in his 'Instructions for the Fathers of our Society who shall be sent to the Hurons', written in 1637.

> The Fathers and brethren whom God shall call to the holy mission of the Hurons ought to exercise careful foresight in regard to all the hardships, annoyances, and perils that must be encountered in making this journey in order to be prepared betimes for all emergencies that may arise.
>
> You must have sincere affection for the savages—looking upon them as ransomed by the blood of the son of God and as our brethren with whom we are to pass the rest of our lives.
>
> To conciliate the savages, you must be careful never to make them wait for you in embarking.
>
> You must provide yourself with a tinder-box or with a burning mirror or with both to furnish them fire in the day-time to light their pipes, and in the evening when they have to encamp; these little services win their hearts.
>
> You should try to eat their sagamite or salmagundi in the way they prepare it, although it may be dirty, half-cooked, and very tasteless. As to the other numerous things which may be unpleasant, they must be endured for the love of God without saying anything or appearing to notice them.
>
> It is well at first to take everything they offer, although you may not be able to eat it all; for when one becomes somewhat accustomed to it, there is not too much . . . .
>
> You must be prompt in embarking and disembarking; and tuck up your gowns so that they will not get wet and so that you will not carry

either water or sand into the canoe. To be properly dressed, you must have your feet and legs bare; while crossing the rapids you can wear your shoes and in the long portages even your leggings.

> You must so conduct yourself as not to be at all troublesome to even one of these barbarians . . . .
>
> Be careful not to annoy anyone in the canoe with your hat; it would be better to take your nightcap. There is no impropriety among the savages.
>
> Do not undertake anything unless you desire to continue it; for example, do not begin to paddle unless you are inclined to continue paddling. Take from the start the place in the canoe that you wish to keep . . . .
>
> Finally, understand that the savages will retain the same opinion of you in their own country that they will have formed on the way; and one who has passed for an irritable and troublesome person will have considerable difficulty afterwards in removing this opinion. You have to do not only with those of your own canoe, but also (if it must be so stated) with all those of the country; you meet some today and others tomorrow who do not fail to inquire from those who brought you what sort of man you are. It is almost incredible how they observe and remember even the slightest fault. When you meet savages on the way, as you cannot yet greet them with kind words, at least show them a cheerful face and thus prove that you endure gaily the fatigues of the voyage. You will thus have put to good use the hardships of the way, and have already advanced considerably in gaining the affection of the savages. (JR XII, 117-21)

Father Brébeuf spent two periods in Huronia—from 1626 to 1629 and from 1634, when he was superior, until 1642—before he arrived for the last time in 1644. When the Iroquois attacked Saint-Louis on 16 March 1649, he was visiting Gabriel Lalemant, who had become the mission priest there. (Lalemant had been at Sainte-Marie since September.) The two priests were captured, taken to Saint-Ignace, hideously tortured, and burned at the stake.

> Father de Brébeuf had his legs, thighs, and arms stripped of flesh to the very bone. I [Christophe Regnault] saw and touched a large number of great blisters, which he had on several places on his body,

from the boiling water which these barbarians had poured over him in mockery of Holy Baptism. I saw and touched the wound from a belt of bark, full of pitch and resin, which roasted his whole body. I saw and touched the marks of burns from the collar of hatchets placed on his shoulders and stomach. I saw and touched his two lips, which they had cut off because he spoke constantly of God while they made him suffer.

I saw and touched all parts of his body, which had received more than two hundred blows from a stick. I saw and touched the top of his scalped head; I saw and touched the opening which these barbarians had made to tear out his heart. . . . (JR XXXIV, 35)

In 1638 Brébeuf had been succeeded as superior of the Huron mission by Jérôme Lalemant, who founded Saint-Marie the next year. The uncle of Gabriel, Jérôme wrote the *Relations* concerning the Hurons for the years 1639 to 1644. He did not remain at Sainte-Marie exclusively but moved about among the other missions, leaving in charge, at various times, Fathers Isaac Jogues, François Du Peron, Pierre Chastellain, Pierre Pijart, or François-Joseph Le Mercier. Le Mercier arrived in Huronia on 13 August 1635, using first Ihonatiria, and in 1637 Ossossané, as his base. He witnessed the Indians' violent reactions as their illnesses multiplied, and once he was attacked. In 1639 he joined Fathers Lalemant and Jogues at the founding of Sainte-Marie, where he stayed for the ten years of its life, overseeing its administration and training and supervising the *donnés* and servants.

After Jérôme Lalemant returned to Quebec in 1645, he was succeeded at Sainte-Marie by Father Paul Ragueneau, who had arrived in the Huron country in 1637 at the height of the epidemic. Continuing the *Relations*, Ragueneau described the Iroquois attacks (having presided at the funeral of Brébeuf and Lalemant in 1649), the destruction of Sainte-Marie, and the failure of Sainte-Marie II on Saint-Joseph Island. It was he who supervised the return to Quebec.

Father Jogues arrived at Saint-Joseph in September 1636. Posted to Sainte-Marie at its inception, he was entrusted with overseeing the erection of the palisade in the summer of 1639. He left Sainte-Marie for Quebec in June 1642. On his way back to Huronia he was captured by Iroquois on the St Lawrence and tortured. He escaped from them in 1643 but was captured again in 1646 and killed, with Jean de La Lande, in what is now New York State. Like Fathers Brébeuf and Lalemant,

Jogues and La Lande are martyr-saints.

The first martyr-saint, René Goupil, was a Jesuit surgeon. He was captured while on his way to Huronia and killed by an Iroquois in September 1642. The martyr-saint who was the first to be killed in Huronia was Antoine Daniel, who arrived in 1634 with Father Brébeuf and was killed at Teanaustayé in 1648. Noël Chabanel, who arrived in 1643, was slain by a Huron on his way to Saint-Joseph Island in December 1649. Charles Garnier, who arrived in 1636, established a mission at Saint-Jean on Georgian Bay and was killed by Iroquois there in December 1649.

The priests were assisted in their work at Sainte-Marie by a few lay brothers—men who were full-fledged Jesuits except for the fact that they chose not to be ordained. They relieved the priests of day-to-day tasks of administration so that they could devote their time to instructing the Indians and also practised a trade. Although lay brothers could not celebrate Mass or administer sacraments, they often assisted at services.

There were five lay brothers at Sainte-Marie: Dominicus Scot, a tailor, who arrived in 1640 and left for France five years later; Ambroise Broult, a cook, who arrived the year Scot left; Louis Gauber, a blacksmith, who arrived in 1642; Pierre Masson, the gardener and replacement tailor, who arrived in 1646, to be followed two years later by Nicolas Noircler, about whom very little is known.

More important to Sainte-Marie than the lay brothers were the *donnés* ('given men'), some of whom were skilled craftsmen. They dedicated themselves to useful mission work but had not taken vows and so were able to carry arms (unlike the lay brothers). Furthermore, they could do other things the lay brothers did not do, such as carrying loads and performing various menial domestic chores.

We by these presents, accept [Jean Guérin] as Donné in the capacity of a Domestic Servant during his lifetime . . . promising, on our part, to maintain him according to his condition with food and clothing, without other wages or claims on his part, and to care for him kindly in case of sickness, even to the end of his life, without being able to dismiss him, in such case, except with his own consent; provided that, on his part, he continue to live in uprightness, diligence and fidelity to our service. . . . 19 March 1642. (JR XXI, 303)

6 Entrance

7 *(over)* Northcourt. Left to right: blacksmith's shop, carpenter's shop, Chapel of St Mary, refectory, cookhouse

A similar agreement was signed by Robert Le Coq in December 1639, though he had first arrived among the Hurons in 1634. He travelled back and forth between Sainte-Marie and Quebec, where he did business on behalf of the priests. On a trip to the northwest in 1639 he took ill with smallpox and was abandoned by the Indians on a rock, where he lay for days until he was rescued. He supervised the buildings and equipment at Sainte-Marie until he left for the last time in 1649 to get help. He was killed by Iroquois near Trois-Rivières in 1650.

Another *donné* was Christophe Regnault, remembered today for his account of recovering the mutilated bodies of Brébeuf and Gabriel Lalemant. He was a shoemaker by trade, and arrived at Sainte-Marie in 1639. Charles Boivin, a *donné* who was a master builder, also arrived the first year, along with Joseph Molère, a skilled nurse and pharmacist; Guillaume Couture, Sainte-Marie's first carpenter; and Jacques Levrier, a shoemaker. Boivin oversaw the building of Sainte-Marie and is believed to have directed the construction of the impressive fireplaces and other stonework that formed the defence bastions before the stonemason, Pierre Tourmente, arrived in 1647. Boivin stayed at Sainte-Marie until it was destroyed in 1649 and moved to Saint-Joseph Island. Later in his life, while living at Quebec, he planned and supervised the construction of a number of religious buildings there and in Montreal, remaining a *donné* until he died in old age.

Other *donnés* were Eustache Lambert, a farmer, and François Gendron, a doctor. Hearing of the dangers facing him on his journey to Sainte-Marie, the pious Gendron told a colleague: 'If my designs tended only to the earth, your words would give me terror; but my heart, desiring only God, fears nothing more.' The priests had requested a doctor when the smallpox epidemic was rising to its height, but by the time Gendron arrived he could do little to help, since it was not known how the disease was transmitted. Nevertheless Gendron toiled on, doing his best. Father Ragueneau wrote that he 'ministered to both the French and the Indians with extraordinary charity in all their sicknesses. He performed excellent cures, in number. He lived with great humility, and practised every virtue, without wages, without gain, purely for the love of God.' When the Sainte-Marie mission failed, Gendron returned to France, where he studied for the priesthood; he was ordained in 1652 at the age of thirty-four. Though it was forbidden for a priest to practise medicine, he did so with papal authority. Through his research and revolutionary treatments, he gained an international reputation, treating both royalty and the poor.

Jacques Douart arrived in 1642 at the age of sixteen and worked as a labourer, but four years later he signed the *donné*'s agreement. Killed by two renegade Hurons in April 1648, he became the only European to die at Sainte-Marie. He was buried in the the cemetery next to the Church of St Joseph.

There were always several young boys at Saint-Marie, some of them orphans, who helped with the chores. Two were Jean and Mathieu Amiot, brothers who became skilled in Indian languages. Jean drowned off Trois-Rivières in 1648, when he was about twenty-three.

More likely a soldier than a *donné*, Médard Chouart des Groseilliers — who later, with his brother-in-law Radisson, became an explorer and one of the originators of the Hudson's Bay Company — was at Sainte-Marie in 1646.

In early 1649 there were 18 priests, 4 lay brothers, 22 *donnés*, 11 domestics (who were paid), 4 boys, and 6 soldiers in the Huron country.

THE HURONS

The Hurons called themselves Ouendat (When-dat), meaning 'islanders' or 'dwellers of a peninsula'. The name Huron was given to the Ouendat by the French because Huron braves sometimes shaved the sides of their heads, leaving a band of hair down the middle. It reminded the French of the bristles on the head of a boar—in French, *hure*. *-on* meant people or men. The Hurons called their country Ouendake (When-da-kay), meaning 'in the islands' or 'a land apart'. The French referred to it as 'Pays des Hurons', meaning land or country of the Hurons: thus the mission was 'Sainte-Marie-aux-pays-des-Hurons'. The word Huronia was not coined until the nineteenth century.

The Hurons were part of the linguistic group of Iroquoian Indians, although the five nations of the Iroquois who lived south of Lake Ontario were longtime enemies. Before the French came, the Hurons lived in twenty to twenty-five villages in an 800-square-mile area between Lake Simcoe and the eastern shores of Georgian Bay. The confederacy was composed of four tribes: the Bear tribe, the largest, lived in the extreme west; next was the Cord; then the Deer; and in the east the Rock. Although these tribes were interrelated, they carried on their business affairs independently of one another and came together only for special feasts, ceremonies, or war.

One of the largest villages, Cahiagué of the Rock tribe, was thought to have 4,500 to 5,000 inhabitants in the early 1600s. Huron villages were generally located on high ground, near a creek or spring, and the main ones were fortified with a protective palisade of saplings laboriously felled with stone axes in the nearby forest. They were abandoned only when firewood and soil were depleted, when the village was in danger of being attacked, or when it burned down. The largest villages had about fifty longhouses, some of them more than 100 feet in length. They were constructed by placing elm bark over a frame of saplings tied together with smaller branches and strips of cedar bark. Each longhouse was inhabited by eight to ten families related through the female line. They formed a clan, headed by a civil chief and a war chief to represent it on tribal and confederacy councils. A number of clans made up a tribe.

Corn was the staple food. It has been estimated that the Hurons must have had 23,300 acres under cultivation to feed the population, and to provide a surplus to cover famine years and for trade with other tribes. One of the first Recollet missionaries in Huronia, Gabriel Sagard, wrote that it was easier to get lost in the Huron cornfields than in the forests.

The Hurons traded surplus corn with neighbouring Neutral and Petun tribes for dried fish and meat, tobacco, and wampum; and with Algonkin tribes as far away as Lake Nipissing for beaver, deer, highly prized black squirrel skins, and copper and charms. All trade was dominated by, and carried out in, the language of the Hurons.

Clearing the land for cultivation was the responsibility of the men, but the women planted and tended the corn, squash, and beans. Because the fields were often many miles from the villages, women and children usually lived in temporary shelters near the fields during the summer, while the men went away hunting, fishing, or to fight.

War was waged on other confederacies for three main reasons: for young braves to gain prestige as courageous warriors; to capture prisoners who would either be sacrificed to a spirit or adopted by a family who had lost a relative in war; or to avenge a murder, which could initiate a lengthy blood feud. Occasionally treaties between warring confederacies were negotiated to arrange for the exchange of prisoners.

Game was already scarce in Huronia in the early 1600s, so hunting parties ranged far to the south and east. Fishing was a more important source of food because of the proximity to Georgian Bay and numerous rivers and smaller lakes. (The Bear tribe had fishing weirs constructed in the narrows between Lakes Couchiching and Simcoe.) Fish and meat were dried and smoked on racks over fires. (Meat was usually reserved for feasts and celebrations, which occurred most often during winter and spring.) The primary food was a soup called sagamité that was made by grinding kernels of corn into coarse meal and throwing it—along with bits of dried or fresh meat, fish, squash, pumpkin, or berries—into a clay pot containing water. Then small stones heated in the fire were placed in the pot to boil the mixture. Family members ate directly from the pot.

For the Hurons everything was inhabited by spirits—some good, some bad—and they were acknowledged in various ways. Dreams were considered to be of great importance because they put the Indians in touch with the spirits, while myths and legends attempted to explain them. The Hurons frowned on the accumulation of wealth as an end in itself and praised generosity and the sharing of possessions. Courting rituals involved sexual intimacy before a woman decided to accept a suitor. Marriage, although easily broken, was monogamous and children were especially loved and well cared for.

On the whole the Hurons were not impressed by the French, considering themselves wiser and more intelligent. They thought the French were physically inferior, and ugly because of their excessive hairiness; the Indians particularly despised beards, which they believed reduced a person's intelligence. They also looked down on the French for depending on them, which the Jesuits certainly did when they first confronted the wilderness. The French quickly adopted Indian moccasins and practical clothing. They had to learn to manage the birch-bark canoe of the Hurons, to snowshoe, shoot rapids, fish through the ice, and eat sagamité. The Jesuits had to learn some of these things too, and to master the Huron language. Nevertheless they saw themselves as superior to the natives because they considered their civilization and technology to be more advanced. And above all because they were Christian. However, their sense of superiority did not prevent them from making far more accommodations to the Huron way of life—that of a well-developed society not subject to easy change—than the Hurons did to Jesuit practices and beliefs.

8 Interior of Boivin building

9 Boivin building

THE RECONSTRUCTION

The first modern reference to the site of Sainte-Marie appears in an Indian treaty of 1789 and refers to 'certain French ruins', which would have been the stone bastions. In 1855 a Jesuit priest, Father Félix Martin, found the area heavily overgrown with trees and the bastions still standing. He was able to clear away enough of the brush to follow the line of what had once been the two stone walls that joined three of the bastions. Thirty years later, pillaging by farmers and relic hunters had reduced bastions and walls to heaps of broken stone. The property became farmland in the late nineteenth century and changed hands several times. In the 1930s James Playfair, a sportsman, had a hunting lodge and stables in what is now Southcourt. The property changed hands again and in 1940 it was purchased by the Society of Jesus, which owns it today.

More than three hundred years after Sainte-Marie had been destroyed, the Ontario government undertook to have it reconstructed as a heritage project for Canada's centennial year. This was accomplished under the direction of Wilfrid Jury, who was then curator of the Museum of Indian Archaeology at the University of Western Ontario.

The plans for much of the reconstruction were based on information gleaned from two archaeological excavations of the site. The first took place in 1941 under the direction of Kenneth E. Kidd, then with the Royal Ontario Museum, when part of the area now known as Northcourt was revealed. Kidd did more work in 1942 and 1943. Between 1948 and 1951 Jury led a team that uncovered the rest of Northcourt, and evidence of Southcourt and the Indian Compound, including the waterway, the church, and the cemetery.

Remains of the bastions and of the low stone walls that lay between them identified part of the outline of Northcourt, but as the wooden buildings of Sainte-Marie had burned to the ground, excavators had to rely on what was below ground, or fell into depressions such as ditches or cellars, for clues about the shape and location of buildings. Post moulds—stains of rotted wood in the soil—were the most easily identified findings. Objects indicated the use of some of the buildings. For example, where a blacksmith shop has been reconstructed, Kidd found metal scraps, a blacksmith's hammer, and thirteen iron axes; Jury found twelve more axes, nails and spikes, and some metal slag and shavings. Jury excavated the site of the carpenter's shop, where he found evidence of planes, a broadaxe, an adze, a scratch awl, and the charred remains of

a work bench. He found that the floor had been clay sprinkled with sand and covered with elm bark, bark side down. Where the cookhouse was reconstructed Jury found many items in the cellar: forks and a fish-hook, bones of cows, pigs, chickens, elk, woodchuck (all boiled and most sawn), fish bones and scales, and kernels of corn that had been carbonated.

Another discovery made by Jury, based on post moulds, was the main building type: a double wall, called *en colombage*—two sets of horizontal planks about six inches apart and held in place by two huge upright timbers placed every eight or ten feet. The space between the planks was filled with insulation of clay and stone. Holes were drilled through the timbers and planks and wooden dowels were hammered into them to hold the structure together. (This was a style of building that was used briefly in Normandy until it was found that the moist clay rotted the wood and caused fast deterioration.)

The excavation of a trench that was thought to be a waterway system was begun by Kidd. In continuing this work Jury uncovered in the east-west channel timbers and planks that appeared to be the gates of three locks. The trench had been lined with upright logs and the depressions of two open basins were found. This narrow waterway, which Jury interpreted as a canal, is about four feet wide and could receive only a small two-man canoe. For this reason the canal theory is not known for certain to be correct.

Originally the waterway was fed by an elaborate aqueduct system that directed water from natural springs in the hill north of Sainte-Marie into the interior of the settlement. Hollowed-out cedar logs were placed end to end in a trench; the top was probably covered over by flat stones and the aqueduct was buried. It surfaces once near the northeast corner of Northcourt inside the palisade and then goes underground again until it empties into the beginning of the north-south waterway. Excavations uncovered a large number of these troughs which, being cedar, were well preserved.

Turning south from the canal, the crew uncovered the remains of three buildings in the area now known as Southcourt. Two seemed to have no special features, but the third differed from all the others at Sainte-Marie. It was constructed of upright cedar logs and the cracks between the logs were chinked with mortar both inside and outside. Given the fact that this style of architecture—called *en pilier*—was common in

10   Chapel of St Mary in Northcourt

11a   Church of St Joseph, Indian
Compound

11b   Elm-bark roof of church

11c   Roofs of chapel and carpenter's
shop in Northcourt

11d   Rear of chapel and its
cedar-shake roof from Southcourt

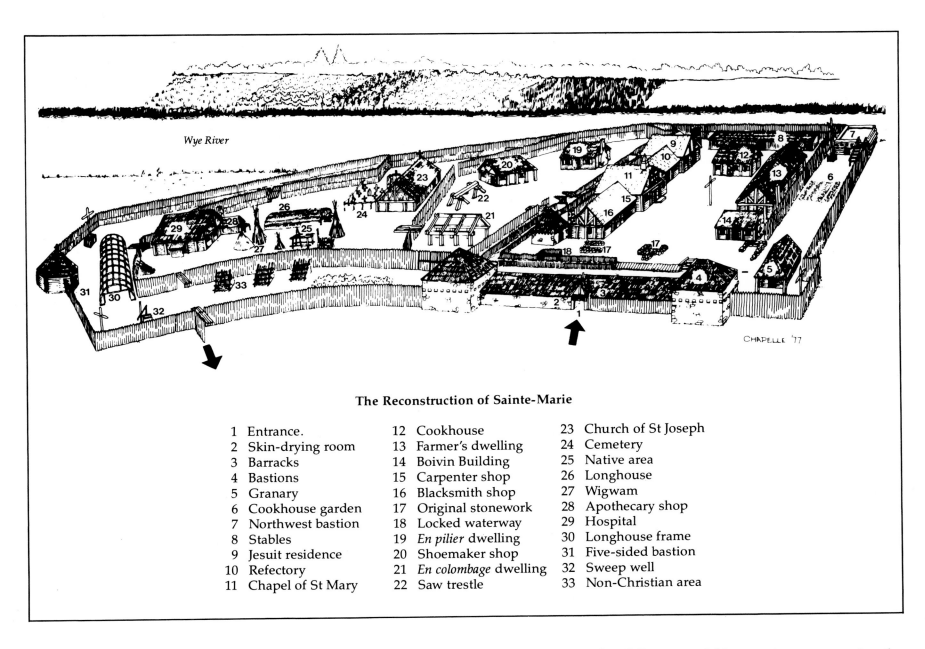

Wye River

CHAPELLE '77

The Reconstruction of Sainte-Marie

1 Entrance.
2 Skin-drying room
3 Barracks
4 Bastions
5 Granary
6 Cookhouse garden
7 Northwest bastion
8 Stables
9 Jesuit residence
10 Refectory
11 Chapel of St Mary

12 Cookhouse
13 Farmer's dwelling
14 Boivin Building
15 Carpenter shop
16 Blacksmith shop
17 Original stonework
18 Locked waterway
19 *En pilier* dwelling
20 Shoemaker shop
21 *En colombage* dwelling
22 Saw trestle

23 Church of St Joseph
24 Cemetery
25 Native area
26 Longhouse
27 Wigwam
28 Apothecary shop
29 Hospital
30 Longhouse frame
31 Five-sided bastion
32 Sweep well
33 Non-Christian area

France and could be erected quickly, it has been theorized that this might have been the first building at Sainte-Marie — the 'single house' Jérôme Lalemant mentions as having been built in 1639.

In the summer of 1950 Jury turned his attention to excavating the Church of St Joseph. The floor of the building, 70 feet by 27 feet, had been hard-packed white sand — there was no planking; the floor was left uncovered because the Indians believed plank floors trapped spirits. Two fireplaces—scarce in churches of the period—and a door only three feet high were two of its features. It appeared that, in order to make the Indians feel at home, a low entrance was provided because the Hurons were accustomed to crouch to enter a longhouse; and not one but two fireplaces provided welcome warmth while they learned the Catechism.

Adjacent to the church Jury found the cemetery, which contained the remains of twenty-three people in twenty-one graves. In one case it appeared that a small child had been buried with the mother in one grave. In another grave the remains of two skeletons were found. A man had been buried according to Christian tradition but beside him was a small bundle of female bones, wrapped in skins according to Huron tradition. It is possible that the man converted to Christianity after his wife's death and, before he died himself, asked that his wife's remains be placed beside him. All burials in the cemetery, with the exception of the female bones, were Christian.

The most significant grave found at Sainte-Marie was not excavated by Jury. In August 1954 Father Denis Hegarty, S.J., an archaeologist, excavated a section of the church floor and discovered the grave site of St Jean de Brébeuf. Proof came in the way of nails forming the shape of a very large coffin—Brébeuf had stood more than six feet tall—and a small iron plaque bearing the inscription:

P. Jean de Brébeuf
Bruslé par les Iroquois
le 17 de mars l'an
1649

'Fr. Jean de Brébeuf/Burnt by the Iroquois/on the 17th of March in the year/1649.' In all the reports of the death of Brébeuf the date is given as March 16th. It seems probable that when the bodies of Lalemant and Brébeuf were retrieved from Saint-Ignace and buried at Sainte-Marie, the story of their deaths was not fully known. The plaque is now on display in the Sainte-Marie Museum.

Archaeological exploration of the remainder of the Indian Compound revealed the outlines of a longhouse, potsherds, ash beds from hundreds of fires, the circular outline of a structure similar to an Alongkin wigwam, and the postmoulds of the hospital. All that remained to be excavated was the non-Christian Indian Compound which offered, among other things, a second longhouse, a few lean-to shelters, a well, and the remains of a five-sided bastion that guarded the southern approach to the settlement.

Searching for information to add to what had been culled from the excavations before the reconstruction began, Elsie McLeod Jury, the Director of Research, studied drawings in European archives and museums as well as buildings that were erected in Sainte-Marie's time and were still standing in France. By comparing excavation data with building methods used in France, the Jurys were able to conceive the probable appearance of Sainte-Marie.

The reconstruction began in 1964. Three years later—after the expenditure of thousands of hours of research, back-breaking labour, and more than a million dollars—a reasonable facsimile of Sainte-Marie stood on the original site. Given the historical evidence that was available, the lack of concrete evidence provided by the seventeenth-century residents and builders, and the fact that the buildings we see today may not all have existed at one and the same time, it is thought to be a convincing simulation of Sainte-Marie in its prime. It was the first major attempt in Canada to preserve our heritage by re-creating the symbols of it.

SAINTE-MARIE TODAY

The reconstructed Sainte-Marie covers almost three acres and is basically triangular in shape. Enclosed by a tall palisade, it lies parallel to the Wye River, with its broad end on the north and its south end bordered by the Wye Marsh. There are three sections—Northcourt, Southcourt, and the Indian Compound—divided by palisades in which gated openings permit easy access from one area to another.

The main entrance, on the northeast side, is centred in a long narrow structure containing a skin-drying room on the left and a barracks on the right. Flanking it is a pair of two-storey stone bastions. (Used for storage, they also provided vantage points from which the countryside to the east could be seen.) After passing through the entrance and crossing over the covered aqueduct that feeds the canal system, visitors enter the spacious Northcourt and see two rows of buildings, one on either side. On the left are the blacksmith and carpenter shops (in one building), and

12 Northwest cross, one of the four crosses marking each corner of the site

the Chapel of St Mary, with the priests' refectory and residence next to it. Across from them is a small dwelling called the Boivin building—named after the *donné* Charles Boivin—and the long granary and farmer's dwelling.

The imposing two-storey Chapel of St Mary dominates Northcourt. Its steeple is topped by a cock, which at the time of Sainte-Marie was a symbol of the denial of Christ by Simon Peter and represented vigilance. Lalemant referred to 'the beauty of our Chapel (which is looked upon in this country as one of the wonders of the world, although in France it would be considered but a poor affair)'. The heavy front doors open into one large room, virtually empty because benches and fireplaces were not permitted in churches in the seventeenth century. The main focus of this room is the altar; beyond it is the sacristy—a partitioned area used for storing vestments and vessels for Mass. Appointments are simple: beeswax candles, a plain wooden tabernacle for the Blessed Sacrament, white linen altar cloths trimmed with lace, wooden crosses marking the fourteen stations, a silver sanctuary lamp, a few religious pictures. Iron braziers, filled with red-hot coals, warmed priests celebrating Mass in winter. When more space was needed for public devotions a second, larger church was built in the Indian Compound, and the altar decorations of St Mary's Chapel were probably transferred there. St Mary's then became a private chapel for the priests' devotions.

Fire was a dreaded danger at Sainte-Marie. Buckets of sand, and possibly water in summer, were kept at strategic locations around the mission. In some buildings the fire hazard was so great there was no fireplace at all: the carpenter's shop, for instance, had a bark floor that was covered with several inches of sawdust and wood shavings. Dimly lit by three small windows, it stands between the blacksmith's shop and the chapel. Tools such as axes, hammers, and planes line the walls and cover workbenches. The carpenter and his apprentice were among the most important labourers at Sainte-Marie, cutting and squaring timbers, sawing planks, making furniture, and whittling eating utensils. Their work is demonstrated by 'interpreters' on the site.

The carpenter's shop was warmed to some extent by the blacksmith's shop next door, which always had a huge roaring fire to keep the forging iron red hot. Working bare to the waist and wearing a large leather apron, the blacksmith kept the iron edges of tools sharp and created door and window hinges, nails by the thousands, candlestick holders, iron utensils, and other such items. A young man who wished to learn this trade had to apprentice for about six years and might have spent the first year just learning how to operate a bellows. Sainte-Marie's bellows had two chambers—an invention of the sixteenth century. The double bellows not only pumped more air into the forge but also prevented a situation called 'blowback', whereby inflammable gases from the fire were sucked back into the bellows and caused an explosion.

Across from these buildings is the granary, which held hundreds of bushels of corn. Even at the time the Jesuits abandoned Sainte-Marie, it was estimated that they still had enough corn to last at least three years.

At the end of Northcourt, facing the entrance, is the cookhouse. Here an 'interpreter', dressed in the cotton chemise and light woollen trousers of the period, tells visitors about Ambrose Brouet, the cook at Sainte-Marie, and the kind of food he prepared there. Even on the hottest days the cooking fires at Sainte-Marie blaze, just as they would have done three centuries ago. Often visitors can smell the wonderful aromas of cornbread baking in the hot-coal oven or a roast cooking over the fire—aromas that would have stimulated the taste buds of the Frenchmen but not of any Indians because they didn't like European food and thought herbs and spices made it smell quite bad. Row upon row of corn, sunflowers, herbs, vegetables (pumpkin, squash), and tobacco hang from the rafters. The Jesuits supplemented their basic diet of corn, beans, and squash—which they adopted from the Hurons and grew in the fields across the Wye—with leaf and root vegetables, the seeds of which were imported from France. In addition they learned from the Indians which wild roots and berries were edible.

Besides experimenting with agriculture, the Jesuits practised animal husbandry. Beef, pork, and chickens were kept for feast days. Cows and pigs were housed in the low gloomy stable behind the cookhouse. The body heat of the animals warmed the compact space and moss stuffed into cracks between the logs helped keep out the winds and snow of winter. Fish and game, though not plentiful, offered further variety in their food.

Just south of the blacksmith shop visitors encounter a small stone bastion. A well-worn path winds around it, briefly paralleling the canal. The visitor crosses over the canal at the first of three locks and enters Southcourt.

In the 1600s this waterway was fed by natural springs flowing from the

13 Hammers and square-headed nails in blacksmith's shop

hill guarding the northern approach to the mission. Today the Martyrs' Shrine and a railway track have cut off the flow of water, so that the canal is operated by water pumped into it from the river. Each day—once in the late morning and again in mid-afternoon—the locks are demonstrated for visitors and a two-man birchbark canoe is lowered and raised through the canal.

The building next to the canal represents what is thought to be Sainte-Marie's first house, constructed in the *en pilier* style. It has a large fireplace next to which Dutch bunkbeds have been built into the wall. Its very thin walls would not have provided much insulation against freezing winter temperatures.

Across Southcourt one can see the frame of an unfinished T-shaped building. This is permanently under construction to demonstrate the *en colombage* building technique that Boivin adopted in preference to *en pilier* because the six-inch-thick walls of *en colombage* provided substantially more insulation. Nearby are the saw trestles where labourers would have spent hours at the back-breaking and tedious task of cutting wooden planks from squared timbers. After a tall white pine had been felled in the nearby forest, it was brought back to Sainte-Marie and allowed to dry for a season. Then it was scored and squared with a broadaxe and smoothed with an adze, before being hoisted on top of the six-foot trestles where a framed pit-saw was affixed to one end. Then it was sawed into boards. Two men had to saw up and down steadily for ten hours to produce thirty-two board feet—*two planks.* Though it would be impossible to estimate the number of planks and timbers used in the original settlement, more than ten thousand were needed to reconstruct Sainte-Marie. It must be assumed, therefore, that the Jesuits would have had more than one or two saw trestles operating.

In a third building in Southcourt the work of Sainte-Marie's two shoemakers is demonstrated by an 'interpreter'. The Frenchmen quickly learned to value Indian moccasins over European shoes, which the rough terrain of Huronia soon wore thin.

Progressing south through a palisade gate we come to the Indian Compound and the Church of St Joseph. The original church was built in 1642 and became the first religious shrine north of Mexico when, in 1644, Pope Urban VIII granted a plenary indulgence to pilgrims who visited it. (The document is on display in the Sainte-Marie Museum.) At the east end of the church is a wooden altar and above it a high vaulted ceiling designed to resemble a Huron longhouse. Two of the windows are covered with oiled stretched deerskin. (Formerly all the windows at Sainte-Marie had this covering, though it permits only a little light to enter.) At the west end of the church, on the right as you enter, is its most prominent feature: the gravesite of St Jean de Brébeuf—the only known gravesite of any of the eight North American martyr-saints. Though his bones were actually removed when the priests abandoned the mission in May 1649, this spot is still considered a pilgrimage point for Roman Catholics.

Beside the church is the Christian cemetery, which was established in 1642. The Indians' graves are marked by crosses. The only European to be buried there was Jacques Douart and his grave is marked by a wooden post in the centre of the cemetery. Nearby are a Huron longhouse and an Algonkin wigwam, both covered with bark. Their shapes are very different: the longhouse is like a long cylinder, while the wigwam is small and circular. (The Algonkin were nomadic and their wigwam was designed to be portable.) 'Smoky warmth' are the words Hurons used to describe the interior of their longhouses, and with good reason. When the cooking fires were going, as they were most of the time, the thick smoke hung about eighteen inches off the earthern floor. (Huron women frequently went blind because of the continuous exposure to smoke.) To create a realistic atmosphere in the Sainte-Marie longhouse today the fires are usually kept smouldering. Visitors can poke their noses in to smell the acrid odour of burning wood and feel the sting of smoke in their eyes, or enter to inspect at close quarters the sleeping benches, fires, and cooking posts of the Hurons.

Sainte-Marie's hospital was in the Indian Compound so that the natives had easy access to it. The interior was divided by a seven-foot-high wall across its width; only one of the resulting two large rooms had a fireplace. In the reconstruction two types of beds are represented. Most beds are short, narrow wooden planks raised off the floor; the others are on the ground and this was the kind the Indians preferred. All the beds have 'mattresses' of cedar boughs and some have blankets.

A thirteen-foot-high palisade separates the Christian Indian Compound from the 'place apart' to the east, where the Indians who had not converted stayed. Both Christian and non-Christian Indians used Sainte-Marie like a hotel, remaining for a few days while they took religious instruction, or just observing and then moving on.

14 Blacksmith with apprentice

15 Carpenter and apprentice work
in the carpenter's shop

16a Window hinge

16b Wooden latch

16c Carpenter's tools

16d Door hinges

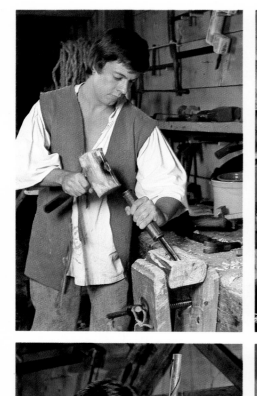

17a Carpenter

17b Shoemaker

17c Blacksmith and apprentice

17d Carpenter with pump-drill

17e Tailor

18 Lining a pit to make pottery

In the non-Christian Indian Compound a second longhouse stands in a state of partial completion to show construction techniques. Here there are several lean-to shelters, a small cultivated area, a sweep well, and the unique five-sided bastion. Two storeys high and with three sides looking out over the Wye Marsh, this wooden bastion provides an excellent defence position commanding the southern approach to the mission.

The last steps of a visit to Sainte-Marie take visitors to the Museum, where they gain a perspective on the settlement and its place in the world. Transporting visitors through a time span from pre-1639 to the present, it features displays on the Jesuits, the Hurons, and what was happening in Europe during the period of Sainte-Marie. The archaeological excavations and reconstruction of the site are the subjects of other exhibits. The Museum has often been called one of the best of its kind in North America.

THE SURROUNDING AREA

In 1640 Father Jérôme Lalemant wrote:

> This place is situated in the middle of the country, on the shore of a beautiful river [the Wye] which, being not more than a quarter of a league in length, joins together two lakes, —one . . . which might pass for a freshwater sea [Lake Huron]; the other, which is toward the South, the contour of which is hardly less than two leagues [6 miles]. (JR XIX, 133-5)

The second lake Lalemant referred to was known as Mud Lake before it shrank into a marsh. It is now part of the Wye Marsh Wildlife Centre, which was established by the Canadian Wildlife Service to interpret the flora and fauna of the surrounding wet and dry lands. The public may tour the Centre, where the unique environment is described by means of displays. They can also explore nature trails or walk far out into the marsh on a boardwalk.

On a hillside overlooking Saint-Marie and the Wye Marsh is the famous Martyrs' Shrine, an impressive twin-spired church that was built in 1926 as a memorial to the men and women, European and Indian, who fostered Christianity in the New World. In particular it honours eight Jesuit martyr-saints, five of whom died in Huronia—Jean de Brébeuf, Gabriel Lalemant, Noël Chabanel, Antoine Daniel, Charles Garnier—and three in what is now New York State: René Goupil, Isaac Jogues, and Jean de La Lande. All were canonized in 1930. The Society of Jesus conducts masses at the Martyrs' Shrine every day from late May to October.

Located near the century-old town of Midland, Sainte-Marie among the Hurons, the Martyrs' Shrine, and the Wye Marsh Wildlife Centre together form Wye Valley Heritage representing the natural, religious, and cultural landscape of an area that is both historically significant and beautiful to behold.

19   Upstairs dormitory of residence in Northcourt

20 Northcourt at twilight

21 Chapel; river and cornfield beyond

22 *Donné* carrying water buckets on a yoke

23   Inside the barnyard

24 Kitchen garden, with granary and northeast bastion

25 Chopping wood in front of cookhouse

26   Inside the cookhouse

27   Feeding chickens

28 North end of canal system
looking south

29 Drawing water from the canal

30   First lock of canal system (east-west)
Entrance to Southcourt on left;
en pilier dwelling in background

31 Entering the landing basin from canal, with second lock in background

32   Interior of *en pilier* dwelling

33   *En pilier* dwelling

34 Squaring timber

35 *En colombage* building under construction in Southcourt

36 Shoemaker's shop

37 Priest in church doorway facing Christian cemetery

38   Superior's quarters in the
residence, Northcourt

39   Celebrating Mass in the Church
of St Joseph

40   Indian Compound: Algonkin wigwam, hospital, longhouse.
Indians stored firewood in these tall triangular stacks

41   Church of St Joseph

42 Building a fire in the Indian Compound

43 Algonkin wigwam and the Church of St Joseph

44 Hospital

45 Inside the longhouse

46 Scything grass in the
non-Christian Compound, with a
lean-to shelter in the background

47 Small garden in the
non-Christian Compound

48 Sweep-well in the
non-Christian Compound

49 Five-sided wooden bastion in
the non-Christian Compound

50 *(over)* Northcourt in winter, from
the river

51   Non-Christian Compound in winter

52   Longhouse frame in non-Christian Compound, southeast cross on left

53 Garden in winter,
non-Christian Compound

54 Cemetery in winter

55 General view at night

56 Brébeuf plaque

DATE DUE

GAYLORD			PRINTED IN U.S.A.